The British Museum

THIS OR THAT?

What Will You Choose at the British Museum?

Pippa Goodhart

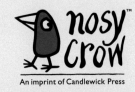
nosy crow

An imprint of Candlewick Press

SKIRT OR SHIRT?

Which clothes would you like to wear?

Can you find clothes with flowers on them?

Can you find some striped pants?

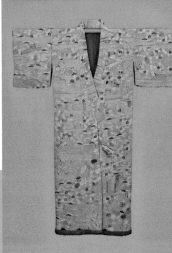

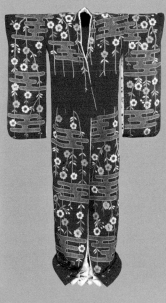

Can you find a hat with feathers?

BRACELET OR BONNET?

Which of these accessories would you like to wear?

How many
pairs of
gloves can
you find?

Can you find some colorful socks?

SANDALS OR SLIPPERS?

Which pair of shoes would you like to wear?

Do you see any shoes with flowers on them?

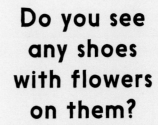

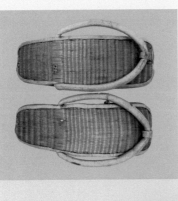

TENT OR TREE HOUSE?

Which building would you like to visit?

Can you find any people in or near the buildings?

Do you see any buildings with a ladder?

Do you
see any
objects with
animals on
them?

CLOCK OR CUP?

Which of these objects would you like in your house?

Which items would you eat with?

CAMEL
OR CAT?

Which is your favorite animal?

How many
animals with
stripes can
you find?

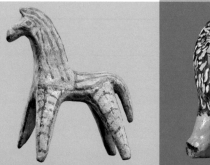

Can you find
an animal
with blue
antlers?

Can you find any creatures that have two heads?

SPHINX OR SERPENT?

Which mythical being do you like best?

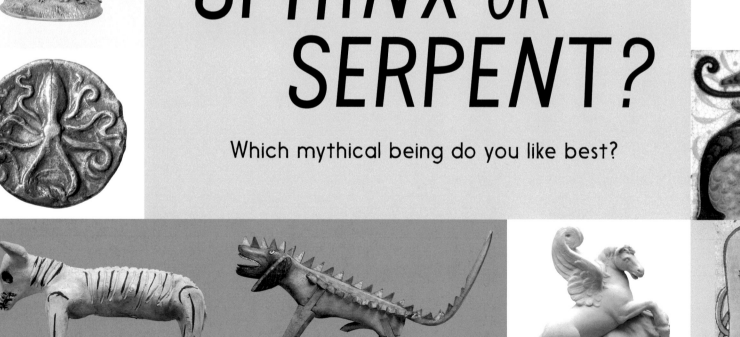

How many
dragons can
you find?

BOAT OR BALLOON?

How would you like to get around?

Which vehicles travel by air?

Do you see any vehicles pulled by animals?

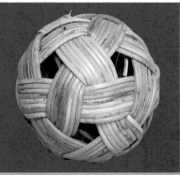

Can you find any toy horses?

DOLL OR DICE?

Which toy would you like to play with?

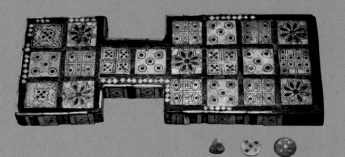

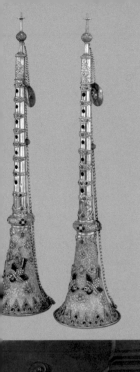

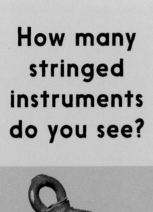

How many
stringed
instruments
do you see?

Can you find someone cutting a cake?

PLUM OR PEAR?

Which of these foods would you like to eat?

How many
pieces of
fruit can you
find?

Can you find a woman watering a plant?

SOLDIER OR SAILOR?

Which of these people would you like to meet?

Who do you see wearing a hat?

Index

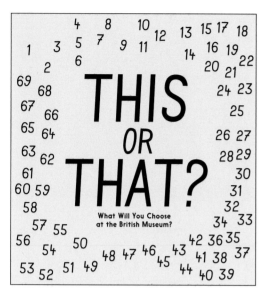

1. Cotton kimono, Japan, 1950–1960 **2.** Toy motorbike, Papantla, Mexico, 1980s **3.** Drum, Dhaka, Bangladesh, 1900–1980s **4.** Leather shoes, Istanbul, Turkey, date unknown **5.** Clay toy tomato, Palugama, Sri Lanka, 1900–1980s **6.** Wooden model airplane, Madagascar, 1980–1985 **7.** Kite, Ahmedabad, India, 1950s–1980s **8.** Model motor car, Bangkok, Thailand, date unknown **9.** Mara helmet, Burma, 1900–1925 **10.** Bamboo and lacquer tumbler, Burma, 1910–1920s **11.** Wooden toy ukulele, Java, Indonesia, 1960s–1975 **12.** Gold and enamel deer figure, Jaipur, India, 1850s–1860s **13.** Cotton wedding dress, Bashindi, Egypt, 1950–1990 **14.** Silver butterfly hairpin, UK, 1800–1830 **15.** Glass scent bottle, Orléans, France, about 1675–1700 **16.** Glazed hippopotamus, Egypt, 2000–1700 BCE **17.** Silk handkerchief, Biba, Egypt, 1900–1927 **18.** Porcelain water-dropper in the shape of a house, Korea, 2000 **19.** Pair of turquoise earrings, Tibet, 1800–1900 **20.** Ceramic vases, Kirman, Iran, 1600–1650 **21.** Goblet-drum, Palestine, 1970s–1980s **22.** Blue glazed shabti, Egypt, date unknown **23.** Goblet, Gateshead, UK, about 1880 **24.** Blue glazed cat, Egypt, 100 CE **25.** Double-headed serpent mosaic, Mexico, 1400–1521 **26.** Green coat with red and purple silk ties, Korea, 1900s **27.** Porcelain teapot, China, 1662–1722 **28.** Earthenware glazed tile, China, 1366–1400 **29.** Porcelain bowl, China, 1723–1735 **30.** Pottery horse figure, Dinajour, Bangladesh, date unknown **31.** Funerary equipment in the form of a model motor car, Penang, Malaysia, 1980s **32.** Kite, Ahmedabad, India, 1950–1980s **33.** Doll made of wax and textile, Puebla, Mexico, 1980s **34.** Clay model banana, Sri Lanka, date unknown **35.** Sunflower badge, UK, 2000–2003 **36.** Porcelain jug, Worcester, UK, date unknown **37.** Camel figurine, Jaipur, India, 1950s–1960s **38.** Toy coconut made of clay, Palugama, Sri Lanka, date unknown **39.** Plastic prayer beads, Saudi Arabia, 1970s **40.** Tambourine, Yemen, 1970s–1980s **41.** Rattan ball, Malaysia, 1800–1900 **42.** Pottery lion toy, Palugama, Sri Lanka, date unknown **43.** Mask made of coconut, Dhaka, Bangladesh, about 1960–1970 **44.** Slippers made of bamboo and leather, Japan, before 1753 **45.** Embroidered hat, Kenya, 1850–1900 **46.** Gold brooch of Helios, Italy, 1860–1870 **47.** Gold earrings, Athens, Greece, 420–400 BCE **48.** Gold llama figure, Peru, about 1500 **49.** Black-figured amphora by The Lysippides Painter, Greece, 520–500 BCE **50.** Model chariot, Tajikistan, 500–301 BCE **51.** Dancer's cotton sash, India, about 1850–1900 **52.** Felt hat, Romania, 1997 **53.** Pair of cotton shoes, Sichuan, China, 1990s **54.** Horse shadow puppet, Thailand, date unknown **55.** Toy clay mouse, Egypt, 1550–1070 BCE **56.** Bronze legionary statuette, location unknown, 101–200 CE **57.** Iron helmet, Sutton Hoo, UK, 600–700 **58.** Toy zebra by Kay Bojesen, Denmark, 1935 **59.** Palm-leaf hat, Andranovolo, Madagascar, 1980–1985 **60.** Key-shaped pilgrim badge, Italy, about 400–1500 CE **61.** Porcelain cat, Jingdezhen, China, 1690–1722 **62.** Earthenware soldier figure, China, 618–906 CE **63.** Polo-style shirt, Nigeria, 2010 **64.** Pottery fish figure, Dhaka, Bangladesh, 1900–1980s **65.** Dove-shaped wooden badge, UK, 1980s **66.** Reindeer and seal boots, Russia, 1990s **67.** Plastic toy oxen, Dhaka, Bangladesh, date unknown **68.** Bamboo and cloth parasol, Burma, 1900–2000 **69.** Pottery cat, Palugama, Sri Lanka, 1900–1980s

---

SKIRT OR SHIRT?

1. Woodblock print by Katsukawa Shun'ei, Japan, 1780s–1790s **2.** Cotton dress, Palestine, 1920s **3.** Beaded waistcoat, Zulu people, KwaZulu-Natal, South Africa, 1950–1987 **4.** Cotton wedding dress, Bashindi, Egypt, 1950–1990 **5.** Green coat with red and purple silk ties, Korea, 1900s **6.** Cotton dress, Malaysia, 1980s **7.** Gouache painting of a woman, India, about 1850 **8.** Polo-style shirt, Nigeria, 2010 **9.** Velveteen waistcoat, Bolivia, early 1980s **10.** Patterned shirt, Manchester, UK, about 1900–1910 **11.** Knitted wool trousers, Atlas Mountains, Morocco, 1968 **12.** Child's dress, USA, before 1923 **13.** Bronze coat of armor, Malaysia, 1700–1860 **14.** Silk skirt, India, 1990s **15.** Cotton flared gown, Maiduguri, Nigeria, 1970s **16.** Cotton kimono, Japan, 1950–1960 **17.** Long-sleeved amuletic coat, Tajikistan, 2013–2014 **18.** Girl's chemise, split skirt, and leggings, Iran, 1880s–1890s **19.** Fragment of tomb painting of Osiris, Egypt, about 1129–1126 BCE **20.** Purple cotton trousers, Iran, 1850s–1900 **21.** Embroidered wedding bodice, Baghdad, Iraq, 1860–1865 **22.** Blouse from a six-piece Hungarian costume, Transylvania, 1940s–1960s **23.** Hand-colored etching titled "A Limb of the Law" by William Holland, UK, 1802 **24.** Dancer's cotton sash, India, about 1850–1900 **25.** Hand-colored etching titled "Mrs Liston as Dollalolla" by George Cruikshank, UK, 1817 **26.** Satin jacket, India, 1980s **27.** Silk kimono, Japan, 1850–1900 **28.** Embroidered gown, Grasslands, Cameroon, about 1920–1930 **29.** Silk-paneled embroidered tunic and trousers, Iran, 1850s–1900 **30.** Persian drawing, Iran, 1650–1700 **31.** Silk kimono, Japan, 1900–1950 **32.** Taffeta silk robe, Iraq, 1890s–1920s **33.** Marble statue, Rome, Italy, 100–150 CE (body), 70–90 CE (head)

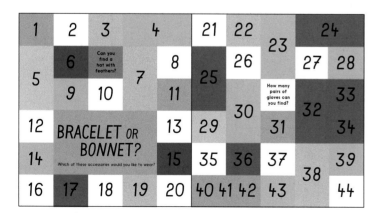

BRACELET OR BONNET?

1. Embroidered hat, Kenya, 1850–1900 **2.** The Snettisham Great Torc, Norfolk, UK, 150–50 BCE **3.** Silver butterfly hairpin, UK, 1800–1830 **4.** Pair of spectacles, China, 1800–1846 **5.** Woollen bag, Cochabamba, Bolivia, date unknown **6.** Cotton bag, Galumpang, Indonesia, 1900–1987 **7.** Woodblock print "Fake Murasaki and the Vestige of Genji" by Utagawa Kunisada II, Japan, 1866 **8.** Wickerwork bag, Mexico, 1980s **9.** Pair of turquoise earrings, Tibet, 1800–1900 **10.** Bamboo and cloth parasol, Burma, 1900–2000 **11.** Gold-cased watch, France, 1774–1780 **12.** Amulet necklace, Egypt, date unknown **13.** Iron helmet, Sutton Hoo, UK, about 550–650 CE **14.** Gold brooch of Helios, Italy, 1860–1870 **15.** Color etching of a figure with flowers by Guy Pierre Fauconnet, France, 1900–1920 **16.** Mara helmet, Burma, 1800–1920s **17.** Bracelet made of beads, Tanzania, Africa, 1800–1900 **18.** Green woollen hat, Transylvania, Romania, 1950–1970 **19.** Engraving of a woman by Pietro Anderloni, Italy, 1800–1849 **20.** Beaded bag, South Africa, 1900–1950 **21.** Turquoise bracelet, USA, 1930–1940 **22.** Palm-leaf hat, Andranovolo, Madagascar, 1980–1985 **23.** Watercolor drawing titled "Schwytz. Costume de femme" by Marcus Dinkel, Switzerland, 1800 **24.** Paper fan, Japan, 1900–1990 **25.** Shoulder shield made of wood, pigment, iron, glass beads, and cloth, Kenya, before 1902 **26.** Belt decorated with beads, Masai people, Kenya, 1980s **27.** Gold earrings, Athens, Greece, 420–400 BCE **28.** Fur gloves, Victoria Island, Canada, 1855 **29.** Turquoise and gold jewelry set, London, UK, about 1850 **30.** Paint-bag made of deerskin, USA, date unknown **31.** Gold helmet, Ur, Iraq, 2600 BCE **32.** Child's bonnet, Nizwa, Oman, 2010 **33.** Hat made from nipa palm leaf, rattan, and bamboo, Sarawak, Borneo, 1950s **34.** Vegetable-fiber hat, Yemen, 1900–1988 **35.** Paper fan, Japan, 1900–1990 **36.** Yakama gloves with beadwork, Washington, USA, mid-1900s **37.** Broad necklace made of beads, Xhosa people, South Africa, 1850–1899 **38.** Square beaded bag, USA, 1700–1800 **39.** Lithograph print titled "Muz Perry" by Hans Strohofer, Germany, 1923 **40.** Brass ring, India, 1800–1860s **41.** Toe-ring, India, 1800–1860 **42.** Brass ring, Sri Lanka, 1700–1900 **43.** Watercolor portrait of a Mughal courtier, India, 1632 **44.** Plastic prayer beads, Saudi Arabia, 1970s

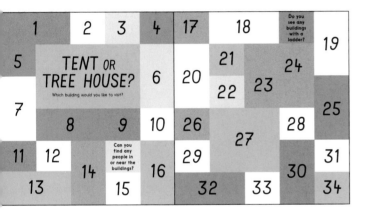

1. Leather shoes, Istanbul, Turkey, 1950s–1960s **2.** Etching of girl standing on the ice by Charles Edouard Taurel, Netherlands, 1844–1894 **3.** Woollen socks, Yauli, Peru, date unknown **4.** Wooden sandals, Burma, about 1990 **5.** Pair of wooden clogs, Netherlands, 1800–2000 **6.** Poster with soldier for shadow puppet theater, Greece, 1930–1970 **7.** Pair of slippers, India, about 1990 **8.** Wooden shoes, Korea, 1800–1900 **9.** Leather slippers with curled toes, India, 1800–1900 **10.** Pair of leather shoes, Albania, 1950–2000 **11.** Model shoes made from paper, Penang, Malaysia, 1900–2000 **12.** Ink and watercolor portrait of Musa Khan, Iran, 1651–1750 **13.** Wooden shoes with pearl-shell, India, probably 1980s **14.** Sandals, Burma, about 1880 **15.** Ceramic shoes, Kirman, Iran, 1600–1650 **16.** Goatskin shoes, Kano, Nigeria, 1970–1974 **17.** Jingly clogs, Aleppo, Syria, 1800–1900 **18.** Wooden bath clogs, Turkey, 1800–1850 **19.** Hand-colored etching titled "The Duchess blush or York Flame" by Isaac Cruikshank, UK, 1791 **20.** Rice-straw sandals, Hinokage, Japan, 1987 **21.** Leather sandals, Wodaabe people, Niger, about 2004 **22.** Leather moccasins, North America, date unknown **23.** Pair of reindeer-skin boots, Norway, 1959 **24.** Embroidered leather boots, Kazakhstan, 1900–1950 **25.** Knitted slippers, Bosnia, 1900–1950 **26.** Beaded boots, Yoruba people, Nigeria, about 1900–1903 **27.** Wooden sandals, Zanzibar, 1920–1927 **28.** Pair of cotton shoes, Sichuan, China, 1990s **29.** Leather slippers with wool appliqué, Berber people, Morocco, about 1969 **30.** Goatskin sandals, Somalia, about 1900–1928 **31.** Leather boots, Kazakhstan, 1800–1900 **32.** Slippers made of bamboo and leather, Japan, before 1753 **33.** Wooden shoes, Afghanistan, 1900–1950 **34.** Dickens, boot and shoemaker's trade card by Folkard, UK, date unknown **35.** Reindeer-skin boots, Finland, 1975 **36.** Reindeer and seal boots, Russia, 1990s

1. Watercolor drawing of a house by John Bewick, UK, 1760–1795 **2.** Brass model of a house, Sumatra, Indonesia, about 1900 **3.** Watercolor painting of the Taj Mahal, India, 1800–1850 **4.** Bamboo model house, Nicobar Islands, India, about 1900 **5.** Bamboo model hut, Nicobar Islands, India, about 1900 **6.** Watercolor drawing of a house by Frederick Nash, UK, 1800–1817 **7.** Watercolor of a tree house, Papua New Guinea, 1900–1950 **8.** Gouache painting of Rama and Sita, India, 1790–1810 **9.** Watercolor drawing of a house by Robert Dixon, UK, 1780–1815 **10.** Porcelain water-dropper in the shape of a house, Korea, 2000 **11.** Woodcut of a mosque by Melchior Lorck, Germany, 1570 **12.** Netsuke palace by Kagetoshi, Japan, 1800–1850 **13.** Watercolor drawing of Harewood House by Thomas Sandby, UK, 1738–1798 **14.** Wooden model house, Nicobar Islands, India, about 1900 **15.** Wood-engraving of a country house by Thomas Bewick, UK, 1778–1828 **16.** Hand-colored aqua-tint titled "The Light-house on Point of Air, Flintshire" by William Daniell, UK, 1815 **17.** Photograph of thatched house, Samoa, Polynesia, 1880 **18.** Woodblock print of houseboat by Shibata Zeshin, Japan, 1847 or 1859 **19.** Sandstone model of temple, India, 1700–1900 **20.** Model rice field house, Java, Indonesia, 1830–1860s **21.** Etching titled "The Mad King's Castle" by Percival Gaskell, UK, 1883–1913 **22.** Painting of "The month of Bhadrapada or Badon", Amber, India, 1700–1725 **23.** Model house by John Gwaytihl, Masset, Canada, 1890s **24.** Model rest house, Burma, 1870s–1880s **25.** Woodblock print of the lighthouse at Tempozan Park by Shumpo, Japan, 1879 **26.** Wood-engraving of a winter scene by Thomas Bewick, UK, 1791–1797 **27.** Watercolor drawing of a house design by Thomas Sandby, UK, 1738–1798 **28.** Palm leaf, wood, and barkcloth model house, Samoa, about 1850 **29.** Watercolor drawing of a windmill by Arthur James Stark, UK, 1831–1902 **30.** Ceramic house by Omar Mahdaoui, Palestine, 1900–2000 **31.** Wooden model house, Singapore, about 1800–2000 **32.** Watercolor drawing of Vine Cottage by Thomas Hosmer Shepherd, UK, 1793–1864 **33.** Etching of a landscape by Francis Vivares, UK, 1739 **34.** Photograph of a lighthouse platform by JM Booth, Brisbane, Australia, 1930s

1. Wooden sewing machine table, Turkmenistan, 1980–1990s **2.** Birch bark cushion, Finland, 2000–2010 **3.** Porcelain teapot, Worcester, UK, 1751–1783 **4.** Porcelain teapot, China, 1662–1722 **5.** Metal teapot, Ladakh, India, 1977 **6.** Copper oil lamp, Sudi, Nepal, about 1980s **7.** Low straight-backed chair, Thebes, Egypt, about 1550–1295 BCE **8.** Wooden fork, Somalia, about 1940–1970 **9.** Wooden spoon, Urumqi, China, 1900s **10.** Silver fish knife, Dusseldorf, Germany, 1916–1917 **11.** Wooden basket, Yuncheng, China, date unknown **12.** Oak longcase clock, Huddersfield, UK, 1775–1785 **13.** Horn comb, Scotland, 1900–1950 **14.** Oval hairbrush by Oomersee Mawjee, Bhuj, India, 1900–1950 **15.** Porcelain vase, China, 1800–1900 **16.** Porcelain bowl, China, 1723–1735 **17.** Wood-engraving of a bookcase by Thomas Bewick, UK, 1782–1783 **18.** Lacquered wood table, Japan, 1800–1900 **19.** Goblet, Gateshead, UK, about 1880 **20.** Bamboo and lacquer tumbler, Burma, 1910–1920s **21.** Water vessel, Somalia, 1900–1930 **22.** Goblet, Egypt, 1077–943 BCE **23.** Silver mirror, place unknown, date unknown **24.** Navajo woven wool blanket, USA, 1860 **25.** Woven food basket, South Africa, 1980–1991 **26.** Bamboo model of a ladder, Andaman Islands, India, 1850–1900 **27.** Wooden broom, Japan, date unknown **28.** Wooden chair, Zambia, about 1900–1940 **29.** Cloisonné jar, China, 1426–1435 **30.** Black-figured amphora by The Lysippides Painter, Greece, 520–500 BCE **31.** Watercolor drawing by John Wykeham Archer, UK, pre-1874 **32.** Model stool made of wood, China, 1800–1900 **33.** Porcelain sugar box, Meissen, Germany, about 1730 **34.** Silk cushion cover, Lebanon, 1980s **35.** Key-shaped pilgrim badge, Italy, about 400–1500 CE **36.** Key, Maldives, 1900–1980 **37.** Model cradle, Armenia, 1900–1950 **38.** Hand-colored lithograph of the Queen's bedroom, UK, 1840 **39.** Striking clock, UK, 1920–1928 **40.** Casket, Limoges, France, about 1180 **41.** Porcelain fish vase, China, 1662–1722 **42.** Woven war rug, Afghanistan, 1979–1989 **43.** Oval mirror by Oomersee Mawjee, Bhuj, India, 1900–2000 **44.** Porcelain jug, Worcester, UK, date unknown **45.** Wooden stool with beaded seat, Kenya, late 1900s or early 2000s

CAMEL OR CAT?

1. Pottery camel, probably Somalia, 1930s **2.** Porcelain swan, Lowestoft, UK, about 1780 **3.** Wooden tiger figure, Mexico, 1980s **4.** Pottery horse figure, Dinajour, Bangladesh, date unknown **5.** Ink sketch of a crab, Japan, 1800–1900 **6.** Etching of a giraffe by Samuel Howitt, UK, 1812 **7.** Pottery dog, Pernambuco, Brazil, mid-1900s **8.** Pottery crocodile, Jalisco, Mexico, 1970s **9.** Toy snake figure, Tlaquepaque, Mexico, 1970s **10.** Porcelain elephant, Japan, 1655–1670 **11.** Toy zebra by Kay Bojesen, Denmark, 1935 **12.** Glazed hippopotamus, Egypt, 2000–1700 BCE **13.** Woodblock print of a kingfisher by Chikuseki, Japan, about 1900 **14.** Terracotta horse figure, Boeotia, Greece, 580–550 BCE **15.** Pottery lion toy, Palugama, Sri Lanka, 1980s **16.** Model lizard, Bangkok, Thailand, 1880–1906 **17.** Gold brooch in the form of a poodle, France, about 1900–1950 **18.** Pottery fish figure, Dhaka, Bangladesh, 1900–1980s **19.** Fish amulet, Ur, Iraq, 2600 BCE **20.** Painted porcelain plaque by Sampson Hancock, Derby, UK, about 1830 **21.** Bronze bull figure, Egypt, about 400–300 BCE **22.** Toy dog by Kay Bojesen, Denmark, 1934 **23.** Watercolor of a bird by Nicolas Robert, France, 1625–1684 **24.** Dove-shaped wooden badge, UK, 1980s **25.** "The Gazi Scroll" Bengal, India, about 1800 **26.** Blue glazed cat, Egypt, 100 CE **27.** Pottery cat, Palugama, Sri Lanka, 1900–1980s **28.** Papercut of fish, China, 1986 **29.** Gold and enamel camel figure, Jaipur, India, 1850s–1860s **30.** Glass vessel, Egypt, 18th dynasty **31.** Watercolor drawing of a bird by Nicholas Robert, France, 1625–1684 **32.** Clay frog figure, India, about 1980 **33.** Watercolor painting of a penguin by John Webber, UK, 1777 **34.** Etching titled "True portrait of the she-antbear" by Andres de le Muela, Spain, 1776 **35.** Gold llama figure, Peru, about 1500 **36.** Porcelain cat, Jingdezhen, China, 1690–1722 **37.** Gold and enamel deer figure, Jaipur, India, 1850s–1860s **38.** Wooden grasshopper figurine, San Antonia Arrazola, Mexico, 1980s **39.** Polar bear figure by Aibilie Innuksuk, Igloolik Island, Canada, 1986

Can you find an animal with blue antlers?

How many animals with stripes can you find?

Which is your favourite animal?

SPHINX OR SERPENT?

1. Wood-engraving of winged dragon by Thomas Bewick, UK, 1778–1790 **2.** Papercut of a dragon, Yangzhou, China, 1985–1995 **3.** Articulated iron dragon by Myochin Kiyohara, Japan, 1700–1900 **4.** Porcelain dish with dragon, China, 1662–1722 **5.** Woodblock print "Newly published collection of masks" by Utatora, Japan, 1863 **6.** Glazed dragon ewer, Vietnam, 1450–1480 **7.** Porcelain dragon vase, China, 1700–1800 **8.** Ivory panel showing sphinx, Iraq, 900–700 BCE **9.** Unicorn standing cup, Nuremberg, Germany, 1579–1605 (head and base), 1800–1898 (body and shields) **10.** Gouache painting of phoenix and dragon, India, 1800–1900 **11.** Wooden tiger figure, Dhaka, Bangladesh, 1980s **12.** Silver coin, Syracuse, Italy, 400–300 BCE **13.** Earthenware tile by William de Morgan, Fulham, UK, 1898–1907 **14.** Skeleton Ox, Ocotlán de Morelos, Mexico, 1970s **15.** Wooden animal figure, Nicobar Islands, India, date unknown **16.** The Pegasus Vase, UK, 1786 **17.** Woodblock print "Newly published collection of masks" by Utatora, Japan, 1863 **18.** Power figure, Bakongo people, Democratic Republic of Congo, about 1875–1905 **19.** Woodblock print "Newly published collection of masks" by Utatora, Japan, 1863 **20.** Papier-mâché figurine, Tlalpujahua, Mexico, 1980s **21.** Woodblock print of storm dragon by Totoya Hokkei, Japan, 1820s–1830s **22.** Papier-mâché dragon figure, Tlalpujahua, Mexico, 1980s **23.** Woodcut of a griffin by Heinrich Petri, Basel, Switzerland, 1544–1552 **24.** Earthenware glazed tile, China, 1366–1400 **25.** Gold plaque ornament from the Oxus Treasure, Tajikistan, 600–500 BCE **26.** Silver bowl cover, Mildenhall, UK, 300–400 CE **27.** Papier-mâché dragon figure, Mexico City, Mexico, 1992 **28.** Double-headed serpent mosaic, Mexico, 1400–1521 **29.** Pair of porcelain lion-dogs, Jingdezhen, China, 1662–1722 **30.** Pottery mermaid figurine, Metepec, Mexico, 1980s **31.** Ogre shadow puppet, Tumpat, Malaysia, about 1950 **32.** Pegasus cast bronze medal by Gottfried Schadow, Germany, 1815 **33.** Linocut of a phoenix by Henry Keen, UK, 1925–1930

Can you find any creatures that have two heads?

How many dragons can you find?

Which mythical being do you like best?

BOAT OR BALLOON?

1. Toy bus made of tin, Palugama, Sri Lanka, 1980s **2.** Gouache painting of Krishna, India, 1790–1810 **3.** Model boat, Chennai, India, 1800–1900 **4.** Part of a panel from a mosaic pavement, Halicarnassus, Turkey, 300–400 CE **5.** Model bullock cart, India, 1800–1900 **6.** Model canoe, Malakula, Vanuatu, date unknown **7.** Wooden model cart, Sri Lanka, about 1850 **8.** Steam train illustration by Perkins & Heath, UK, 1829–1835 **9.** Toy truck, Miakara, Madagascar, early 1980s **10.** Plaited bicycle figurine, Chigmecatitlan, Mexico, 1970s **11.** Wood-engraving of a ship by Thomas Bewick, UK, 1779 **12.** Model chariot, Tajikistan, 500–301 BCE **13.** Ink drawing of a boat, China, 1820 **14.** Model motor car, Bangkok, Thailand, date unknown **15.** Gouache painting of man riding a camel, India, 1800–1850 **16.** Etching titled "How to ride with Elegance thro' the Streets" by James Gillray, UK, 1800 **17.** Funerary equipment in the form of a model motor car, Penang, Malaysia, 1980s **18.** Woodblock print of a Dutch ship, Japan, 1800–1850 **19.** Wooden model airplane, Madagascar, 1980–1985 **20.** Toy helicopter, Vatomasy, Madagascar, early 1980s **21.** Figurine of skeleton man and cart, Puebla, Mexico, 1980s **22.** Cycle rickshaw, Dhaka, Bangladesh, 1980s **23.** Aluminium toy bicycle, Delhi, India, 1991 **24.** Drawing of a procession of the King of Kabul, India, about 1840 **25.** Wood-engraving of man riding wagon by William Dickes, UK, 1830–1892 **26.** Etching titled "View of the ascent of Mr Lunardi's Celebrated air Balloon from the Artillery Ground Sept. 15th 1784" by Thomas Deeble, UK, 1784 **27.** Toy motorbike, Papantla, Mexico, 1980s **28.** Woodblock print by Kawabata Gyokusho, Japan, 1880–1886 **29.** Model motor bus, Mexico City, Mexico, 1980s **30.** Model airplane, Yucatan, Mexico, 1970s **31.** Funerary equipment in the form of a model motor bicycle, Penang, Malaysia, 1980s **32.** Boat model, probably Indonesia, probably 1800s **33.** Wooden figure of a policeman riding a bicycle, Kenya, before 1982 **34.** Watercolor drawing of a coastal scene by Theodore Gudin, France, 1817–1880

Do you see any vehicles pulled by animals?

Which vehicles travel by air?

How would you like to get around?

DOLL OR DICE?

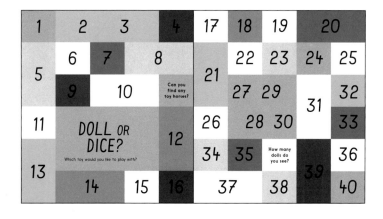

1. Three wooden kokeshi dolls, Sendai City, Japan, probably 1900–2000 **2.** The Lewis Chessmen, Uig, Scotland, 1150–1175 **3.** Wooden cat figure, Thebes, Egypt, about 1550–1069 BCE **4.** Spinning top, Ritabel, Indonesia, 1800–1900 **5.** Paper kite, Cuetzalan del Progreso, Mexico, 1980s **6.** Wooden toy horse on wheels, Akhmim, Egypt, about 1–300 CE **7.** Toy basket, Dhaka, Bangladesh, 1980s **8.** Game box, counters, and dice, Dhaka, Bangladesh, 1980s **9.** Rattan ball, Malaysia, 1950s **10.** Toy clay mouse, Egypt, 1550–1070 BCE **11.** Pottery game-pieces, Egypt, about 1550–343 BCE **12.** Toy catapult, Vezo people, Madagascar, early 1980s **13.** Part of a game made of shell, Johor, Malaysia, 1880s–1910 **14.** The Royal Game of Ur, Iraq, 2600 BCE **15.** Plastic toy oxen, Dhaka, Bangladesh, 1980s **16.** Toy made of paper and wood, Dhaka, Bangladesh, 1980s **17.** Kite, Ahmedabad, India, 1950s–1980s **18.** Toy car, Ladakh, India, 1977 **19.** Toy horse with wheels, Dhamrai, Bangladesh, 1900–1980s **20.** Wooden rattle by Kay Bojesen, Denmark, 1932 **21.** Set of dominoes, Burma, about 1850s–1880s **22.** Woodblock print of children playing a game by Miyagawa Shuntei, Japan, 1896 **23.** Toy cash register, China, 2003 **24.** Linen toy ball, Egypt, 30 BCE–641CE **25.** Stone dice, location unknown, date unknown **26.** Sandstone dice, Egypt, 700–600 BCE **27.** Doll made of acrylic yarn and wire, Lake Titicaca, South America, 1990s **28.** Doll made of wax and textile, Puebla, Mexico, 1980s **29.** Doll made of cloth, Cajamarca, Peru, date unknown **30.** Doll, Huancavelica, Peru, date unknown **31.** Wooden toy, San Antonio de la Isla, Mexico, 1970s **32.** Wooden toy horse, Mexico, 1970s **33.** Playing cards, Orissa, India, 1950s

Can you find any toy horses?

How many dolls do you see?

Which toy would you like to play with?